Anarchism:
Arguments for and against

by

Albert Meltzer

Originally published by Cienfuegos Press,
Orkney, 1981

Published by AK PRESS,
Scotland, 2001

This edition published by Active Distribution
Croatia. 2023

ISBN 978-1-914567-22-3

www.activedistribution.org

Albert Meltzer and the Anarchist idea

The basis of Albert's Anarchism was the idea that working class people have the potential to change society. This put him at odds with the cheerleaders of capitalism; 'revolutionary' parties who wanted to capture state power on behalf of the working class and 'progressive' intellectuals who claimed to have reinvented Anarchism in their own image.

First published in 1981, *Anarchism: Arguments for and against* is the most reprinted of Albert's writings. Albert's first written response to an objector came in *War Commentary* in May 1944. The roots of this text lie in his 1968 pamphlet *Aims and principles of Anarchism: an essay at defining what the Anarchist Movement is and how wide a field it covers*, the book he co-wrote with Stuart Christie *The Floodgates of Anarchy* (published in 1970) and a series of articles on 'objections to Anarchism' in *Black Flag* in the early seventies. This final edition shows how Albert responded as the movement changed around him: he was happy to make room for some feminists, but less impressed with proponents of 'dole autonomy'. *Anarchism: Arguments for and against* even turns up in academic articles, frequently (but not only) as an obstacle to some intellectual innovation.

Albert took writing seriously, as shown by in his vast output of articles and his fulminations against the Fleet Street 'lie machine'. Paul Dacre of the *Daily Mail* said a newspaper columnist should affect their reader: 'Make them laugh, make them cry, or make them angry'. Albert was happy to make people laugh, and not averse to making them angry. Beyond that, *Anarchism: Arguments for and against* says we should hope – but also take steps towards a free society.

KSL Collecive
April 2023

Many more articles by and about Albert are at;

www.katesharpleylibrary.net/

EDITORS INTRODUCTION (2000)

This is the second revised edition of "Anarchism: Arguments For and Against" and was the edition that Albert Meltzer was working on at the time of his death on May 7th 1996. This book was an important one to Albert and it was one whose arguments he came back to often in his other writings.

Albert had become increasingly concerned about what he saw as the ghettoisation of anarchism. Separated from the working class base so necessary to achieve social revolution, anarchism could easily fall into the twin traps of philosophical radicalism or revolutionary arrogance, the "we're more militant than anyone else" approach. Both strands have appeared in British anarchism alongside a sometimes demoralising and destructive incestuous approach to revolutionary change. Anarchists talk only to other anarchists and are unable to relate to the vast majority of people who are not of their belief and see anarchism as a rather exotic or illogical idea.

This then was Albert's attempt to examine arguments people may have about why anarchism can never work and to counter them. He also examines the basic tenets of anarchist thought and practice and in doing so destroys some of the myths that have been created about anarchist theory and action. It's a book for those of us who try to win people over to our ideas in everyday life and as such it is a book that tries to break down the walls of the ghetto that anarchism has become trapped in.

ALBERT MELTZER
Born: London, January 7, 1920.
Died: May 7, 1996, 8:05 a.m.

Albert Meltzer was one of the most enduring and respected torchbearers of the international Anarchist movement in the second half of the twentieth century. His sixty-year commitment to the vision and practice of Anarchism survived both the collapse of the Revolution and Civil War in Spain and the Second World War; he helped fuel the libertarian impetus of the 1960s and 1970s and steer it through the reactionary challenges of the Thatcherite 1980s and post Cold War 1990s.

Fortunately, before he died, Albert managed to finish his autobiography, *I Couldn't Paint Golden Angels*, a pungent, no-punches pulled Schvejkian account of a radical twentieth century enemy of humbug and injustice. A lifelong trade union activist, he fought Mosley's Blackshirts in the battle of Cable Street; played an active role in supporting the Anarchist communes and militias in the Spanish Revolution and the pre-war German anti-Nazi resistance, was a key player in the Cairo Mutiny [after] the Second World War, helped rebuild the post-war anti-Franco resistance in Spain and the international Anarchist movement. His achievements include *Cuddon's Cosmopolitan Review*, an occasional satirical magazine first published in 1965, and named after Ambrose Cuddon, possibly the first consciously Anarchist publisher in the modern sense, the founding of the Anarchist Black Cross, a prisoners' aid and ginger group and the paper which grew out of it – *Black*

Flag. However, perhaps Albert's most enduring legacy is the Kate Sharpley Library, probably the most comprehensive Anarchist archives in Britain.

Born into a mixed marriage in the London of Orwell's *Down and Out* in which there were few homes for heroes but many heroes fit only for homes, Albert was soon enrolled into political life as a private in the awkward squad. His decision to go down the road of revolutionary politics came – he claimed – in 1935 at the age of 15 – as a direct result of taking boxing lessons. Boxing was considered a "common" sport, frowned upon by the governors of his Edmonton school and the prospective Labour MP for the area, the virulently anti-boxing Dr. Edith Summerskill. Perhaps it was the boxers' legs and footwork he acquired as a youth which gave him his lifelong ability to bear his considerable bulk. It certainly induced a lifetime's habit of shrewd assessment of his own and opponents' strength and weaknesses.

The streetwise, pugilistic, and bookish schoolboy also attended his first Anarchist meeting in 1935 where he first drew attention to himself by contradicting the speaker, Emma Goldman, by his defence of boxing. However, he soon made friends with the ageing Anarchist militants of a previous generation and became a regular and dynamic participant in public meetings. The Anarchist-led resistance to the Franco uprising in Spain in 1936 gave a major boost to the movement in Britain, and Albert's activities ranged from organising solidarity appeals to propaganda, working with Captain J.R.White to organise illegal arms shipments to the CNT in Spain – from Hamburg – and acting as a contact for the Spanish Anarchist intelligence service in Britain.

Albert's early working career ranged from fairground promoter, a theatre-hand and occasional film extra. One film in which Albert appeared was Leslie Howard's *Pimpernel Smith*, an anti-Nazi film that did not follow the line of victory but rather of revolution in Europe. The plot called for Communist prisoners, but by the time Howard came to make it in 1940, Stalin had invaded Finland and the script was changed to Anarchist prisoners. Howard decided that none of the actors playing the Anarchists seemed real and insisted that real Anarchists, including Albert, be used for the concentration camp scenes. One consequence of this meeting was Howard's introduction to Hilda Monte, a prominent but unsung hero of the German Anarchist resistance to Hitler, which may have contributed to his subsequent death enroute to Lisbon. Albert's later working years were spent mainly as a second-hand bookseller and, finally, a Fleet Street copytaker. His last employer was, strangely enough, the *Daily Telegraph*.

While by nature a remarkably gentle, generous and gracious soul, Albert's championship of Anarchism as a revolutionary working class movement brought him into direct and sustained conflict with the neo-liberals who came to dominate the movement in the late 1940s. Just as people are drawn to totalitarian movements like fascism and communism because of their implicit violence and ideological certainties, many otherwise politically incompatible people were drawn to Anarchism because of its militant tolerance. Albert was vehemently opposed to the repackaging and marketing of Anarchism as a broad church for academia-orientated quietists and single-issue pressure groups. It was ironical that one of this group should publicly dismiss Anarchism as a spent historical force in 1962, blissfully unaware of the post-Butskellite storm which was about to break and the influence Anarchist and libertarian ideas would have on this and other generations yet to come.

It was his championship of class struggle Anarchism, coupled with his scepticism of the student-led New Left in the 1960s, which earned Albert his reputation for sectarianism. Paradoxically, as friend and *Black Flag* cartoonist Phil Ruff points out in his introduction to Albert's autobiography, it was the discovery of class struggle Anarchism through the sectarianism of *Black Flag* under Albert's editorship that convinced so many Anarchists of his and subsequent generations to become active in the movement. The dynamic and logic of Albert's so-called sectarianism continued to bring countless young people into the Anarchist movement then, and for a further 30 years until his untimely stroke in April 1996.

It is difficult to write a public appreciation of such an inscrutably private man. Albert Meltzer was often like a member of a tug-of-war team. You never quite knew if he was there simply to make up numbers or if he was the anchor-man of the whole operation. To Albert, all privilege was the enemy of human freedom; not just the privilege of capitalists, kings, bureaucrats and politicians but also the petty aspirations of opportunists and careerists among the rebels themselves. Much of what he contributed to the lives of those who knew him must go unrecorded, but he will be remembered and talked about fondly for many years to come by those of us whose lives he touched.

Stuart Christie

Introduction

The Historical Background to Anarchism

It is not without interest that what might be called the Anarchist approach goes back into antiquity; nor that there is an Anarchism of sorts in the peasant movements that struggled against State oppression over the centuries. But the modern Anarchist movement could not claim such precursors of revolt as its own any more than other modern working class theories. To trace the modern Anarchist movement we must look closer to our own times. While there existed libertarian and non-Statist and federalist groups, which were later termed anarchistic retrospectively, before the middle of the nineteenth century, it was only about then that they consciously became what we now call Anarchists.

In particular, we may cite three philosophical precursors of Anarchism, Godwin, Proudhon and perhaps Hegel. None of these was in fact an Anarchist though Proudhon first used the word in its modern sense (taking it from the French Revolution, when it was first used politically and not entirely pejoratively). None of them engaged in Anarchist activity or struggle, indeed Proudhon engaged in parliamentary activity. One of the poorest, though ostensibly objective, books on Anarchism, Judge Eltzbacher's *Anarchism*, (first English language Edition 1907) describes Anarchism as a sort of hydra-headed theory some of which comes from Godwin, some from Proudhon, some from Stirner (another philosopher who never mentions Anarchism) and some from Kropotkin, each a different variation on a theme. The book may be tossed aside as valueless except in its description of what these particular men thought. Proudhon did not write a programme for all time, nor did Kropotkin in his time write for a sect of Anarchists. But many other books written by academics are equally valueless: many professors have a view of Anarchism based on the popular press or from an isolated philosophical reading of Anarchist "classics". Anarchism is neither a mindless theory of destruction nor, despite some liberal-minded literary conceptions, is it hero-worship of people or institutions, however liberated they might be.

Godwin is the father of the Stateless Society movement, which diverged into three lines. One, that of the Revolutionary Anarchists (with which we will deal). Two, that of classic American Individualism, which included Thoreau and his school, sometimes thought of as anarchistic, but which equally gave rise to the 'rugged individualism' of modern 'libertarian' capitalism and to the pacifist cults of Tolstoy and Gandhi which influenced much of the hippy cult.

The third school of descent from Godwin is simple liberalism and, at times, militant liberalism, proponents of which convince themselves that they are the real Anarchists. This third group has done much damage to the Anarchist movement.

The second line of descent from Godwin is responsible for the 'Pacifist Anarchist' approach or the 'Individualist Anarchist' approach that differs radically from revolutionary Anarchism. It is sometimes too readily conceded that 'this is, after all, anarchism'. Pacifist movements, and the Gandhian in particular, are usually totalitarian and impose authority (even if only by moral means); the school of Benjamin Tucker – by virtue of their individualism – accepted the need for police to break strikes so as to guarantee the employer's 'freedom'. All this school of so-called Individualists accept, at one time or another, the necessity of the police force, hence for government, and the definition of Anarchism is no government.

Dealing here with the 'first line of descent' from Godwin, his idea of Stateless Society was introduced into the British working class movement by Ambrose Cuddon (jun). His revolutionary internationalist and non-Statist socialism came along in the late days of English Chartism and reflected sympathy for the French Proudhonians. Those who in Paris accepted Proudhon's theory did not consider themselves Anarchists, but Republicans. They were for the most part self-employed artisans running their own productive businesses. The whole of the French economy was geared both to the peasantry and to the artisan – this, the one-person business of printer, bookbinder, wagon and cart maker, blacksmith, dressmaker, goldsmith, diamond polisher, hat-maker as distinct from the factory or farm worker of the time, who worked for an employer. Independent, individualistic and receiving no benefit from the State but the dubious privilege of paying taxes and having to fight for it they were at that time concerned to discover an economic method of survival that would withstand encroaching capitalism.

Marx described them as 'petty bourgeois', which had a different meaning in the 19th century. He justifiably claimed that these 'petty bourgeois' were not as disciplined as the then factory workers (he despised farm workers) and said that when they were forced into industry they did not faithfully follow the line laid down by a disciplined party from outside the class, but were independent of mind and troublesome to organisation imposed from above, their frustration with events often leading to violence. They moved to Anarchism and via syndicalism spread it through the working class. (This claim is echoed by Marxists nowadays, when the term 'petty bourgeois' means something utterly different – solicitors and chartered accountants – and thus makes Marx's quite sensible analysis sound utterly ridiculous).

These French and English movements came together in the First International. The International Workingmen's Association owed its existence to Marx and indirectly to Hegelian philosophy. But within the International, there was not only the 'scientific socialism' of Marx, but also Utopian Socialism, Blanquism (working class republicanism), English Trade Unionism, German authoritarian and opportunistic socialism, and Spanish, Swiss and Italian stateless socialism, as well as national Republicanism and the various federalistic trends of the time.

Bakunin was not the 'father' of Anarchism, as he has often been described. He was not an Anarchist until late in life. He learned his federalism and socialism from the Swiss workers of the Jura, and gave expression to the ideas of the Godwinian and Proudhonian 'federalists', or non-State socialists. In many countries, Spain and Italy in particular, it was Bakunin's criticism of the ideas of Marx that gave the federalist movement its definition as well as striking a chord with the day to day situation of the people there. The ideas of Bakunin disseminated by activists like Fanelli held up a mirror to the militants in these countries and echoed their private conversations and public struggles.

There had grown up by 1869 a very noticeable trend within the international that was called 'Bakuninist' which was in one line from Godwin and another from Proudhon. When the Paris Commune exploded in the face of the International, it was the parting of the ways (though this was deferred a little longer, and seemed to follow personal lines). From then on Anarchists and Marxists knew by their different analyses, interpretations and actions during the Paris Commune, that they were separate.

All the same, for many years Anarchists continued to form part of the Socialist Movement that included Marxists and Social-Democrats. Marx had not succeeded in building a mass movement. The German socialist movement was more influenced by Lassalle; English socialism by reformist and Christian traditions of radical nonconformity. Only after Marx's death, when Marxism was the official doctrine of German social-democracy, were Anarchists finally excluded from Socialist Internationals; Social Democracy marched on to its own schisms that tore it apart and blurred its identity as conflicts occurred between various factions.

There were no such schisms at that time in the Anarchist movement. Popular opinion made such figures as Tolstoy into (what he never claimed to be) an Anarchist (he was not; neither in the normal sense of the words was he a Christian, nor a Pacifist, as popularly supposed, but his idolators always know better than he). He was though derived from the 'second line' of Godwinism like many other caricature-Anarchists. What we may call 'mainstream' Anarchism was coherent and united, and was given body by the writings of a number of theoreticians, such as Peter Kropotkin, Errico Malatesta, Luigi Galleani and others.

After the bloody suppression of the Paris Commune, and repression in many parts of the world – notably Tsarist Russia, Anarchism passed into its well known stage of individual terrorism. It fought back, and survived, and gave birth to (or was carried forward in) the revolutionary syndicalist movement which began in France. It lost ground after the First World War, because of the revival of patriotic feeling, the growth of reformist socialism and the rise of fascism; and while it made a contribution to the Russian Revolution, it was defeated by the Bolshevik counter-revolution. It was seen in both a constructive and destructive role in the Spanish Revolution of 1936.

By the time of the Second World War, Anarchism had been tried and tested in many revolutionary situations and labour struggles. Alternative forms had been tried and discarded. The German Revolution had introduced the idea of Workers Councils. The experience of the American IWW had shown the possibilities of industrial unionism and how one can 'build the new society in the shell of the old'. In the 'flint against flint' argument against Marxist Communism, the lesson of what socialism without freedom meant in Russia, and the failure of reformist socialism everywhere, we can see the essential truths of Anarchism and the failure of its adherents to win popular support for them.

There were never theoreticians of Anarchism as such, though it produced a number of theoreticians who discussed aspects of its philosophy. Anarchism has remained a creed that has been worked out in action rather than as the putting into practice of an intellectual idea. Very often, a bourgeois writer comes along and writes down what has already been worked out in practice by workers and peasants; he is attributed by bourgeois historians as being a leader, and by successive bourgeois writers (citing the bourgeois historians) as being one more case that proves the working class relies on bourgeois leadership.

More often, bourgeois academics borrow the name 'Anarchism' to give expression to their own liberal philosophies. For some professors and teachers, 'Anarchism' was anything from Tolstoyism to the IRA, from drug taking to militant trade unionism, from nationalism to bolshevism. With the bankruptcy of Marxism now universally recognised, Anarchism has become fair game for those eager to climb on the academic gravy train. Theses abound trying to define, redefine and reshape both Anarchism's doctrines and history to prove an academic point worthy of further study. These studies reflect their writers need for leaders, and the importance they give to writing indicates how incapable many bourgeois academics are in believing in the creative potential of ordinary people. For every Kropotkin there were a thousand like Facerias, for every Rocker a thousand Jack Kieltys.

INALIENABLE TENETS OF ANARCHISM

That People are Born Free

Our rights are inalienable. Each person born on the world is heir to all the preceding generations. The whole world is ours by right of birth alone. Duties imposed as obligations or ideals, such as patriotism, duty to the State, worship of God, submission to higher classes or authorities, respect for inherited privileges, are lies.

If People are Born Free, Slavery is Murder

Nobody is fit to rule anybody else. It is not alleged that people are perfect, or that merely through his/her natural goodness (or lack of same) he/she should (or should not) be permitted to rule. Rule as such causes abuse. There are no superpeople nor privileged classes who are above 'imperfect Humanity' and are capable or entitled to rule the rest of us. Submission to slavery means surrender of life.

As Slavery is Murder, so Property is Theft

The fact that people cannot enter into their natural inheritance means that part of it has been taken from him or her, either by means of force (old, legalised conquest or robbery) or fraud (persuasion that the State or its servants or an inherited property owning class is entitled to privilege). All present systems of ownership mean that some are deprived of the fruits of their labour. It is true that, in a competitive society, only the possession of independent means enables one to be free of the economy (that is what Proudhon meant when, addressing himself to the self-employed artisan, he said "property is liberty", which seems at first sight a contradiction with his dictum that it was theft). But the principle of ownership, in that which concerns the community, still remains at the bottom of inequity.

If Property is Theft, Government is Tyranny

If we accept the principle of a socialised society, and abolish hereditary privilege and dominant classes, the State becomes unnecessary. If the State is retained, unnecessary government becomes tyranny since the governing body has no other way to maintain its hold. "Liberty without socialism is exploitation: socialism without liberty is tyranny" (Bakunin).

If Government is Tyranny, Anarchy is Liberty

Those who use the word "Anarchy" to mean disorder or misrule are not incorrect. If they regard government as necessary, if they think we could not live without Whitehall directing our affairs, if they think politicians are essential to our well-being and that we could not behave socially without police, they are right in assuming that Anarchy means the opposite to what government guarantees. But those who have the reverse opinion and consider government to be tyranny, are right too in considering Anarchy (no government) to be liberty. If government is the maintenance of privilege and exploitation and inefficiency of distribution, then Anarchy is order.

THE CLASS STRUGGLE

Revolutionary Anarchism is based on the class struggle, though it is true that even the best of Anarchist writers, to avoid Marxist phraseology, may express it differently. It does not take the mechanistic view of the class struggle originally taken by Marx and Engels that only the industrial proletariat can achieve socialism, and that the inevitable and scientifically predictable victory of this class represents the final victory. On the contrary: had Anarchism been victorious in any period before 1914, it would have been a triumph for the poorer peasants and artisans, rather than among the industrial proletariat amongst whom the concept of Anarchy was not widespread.

As we have said, Marxists accuse the Anarchists of being petty bourgeois. Using the term in its modern sense, it makes Marx look ridiculous. Marx was distinguishing between the bourgeois (with full rights of citizens as employers and merchants) and the minor citizens – i.e. self-employed workers. When Marx referred to the Anarchists being 'petty bourgeois' he was expressing something that was happening, especially after the breaking up of the independent Communes of Paris and Barcelona, and the breakdown of the capitalist economy, in his day. But, with the change of meaning, to think of today's Anarchists as frustrated bowler-hatted bank managers turning to violence because they have been forced into industry is straining one's sense of the ridiculous.

Marx thought the industrial proletariat was not used to thinking for itself – not having the leisure or independence of the self-employed – and was therefore only capable by itself of developing a 'trade union mentality', needing the leadership of an 'educated class' coming from outside to provide a wider perspective. In his day this leadership was thought of as the scholars, in later times the students. Later in the 1960s the students racked by guilt at not being black, imprisoned or working class tried to bridge this divide. They helped create what the Americans call the

New Left (and were seen by some desperate Marxists as a class in themselves)

Any class may be revolutionary in its day and time; only a productive class may be libertarian in nature, because it does not need to exploit. The industrialisation of most Western countries meant that the industrial proletariat replaced the old 'petty bourgeois' class and what is left of them became capitalist instead of working class, because it had to expand and therefore employ in order to survive. But recent tendencies in some Western countries are leading to the displacement of the working class and certainly the divorcing of them from their productive role. Mining, shipbuilding, spinning, manufacturing industries and whole towns are closed down and people are forced to into service jobs like car park attendants or supermarket assistants which are not productive and so carry no industrial muscle.

When the industrial proletariat developed, the Anarchist movement developed into anarcho-syndicalism, something coming from the workers themselves, contrary to the idea that they needed a leadership from outside the class or could not think beyond the wage struggle. Anarcho-syndicalism is the organisation at places of work both to carry on the present struggle and eventually to take over the places of work. It would thus be more effective than the orthodox trade union movement and at the same time be able to bypass a State run economy in place of capitalism.

Neither Anarchism nor Marxism has ever idealised the working class (except sometimes by way of poetic licence in propaganda!) – this was a feature of the Christian Socialists. Nor was it ever suggested that they could not be reactionary. It would be trying the reader's patience too much to reiterate all the 'working class are not angels' statements purporting to refute that the working class could not run their own places of work. Only in heaven, so I am informed, will it be necessary for angels to take over the functions of management!

ORGANISATION AND ANARCHISM

Those belonging to or coming from authoritarian parties find it hard to accept that one can organise without 'some form' of government. Therefore they conclude, and it is a general argument against Anarchism, that 'Anarchists do not believe in organisation'. But government is of people, organisation is of things.

There is a belief that Anarchists 'break up other people's organisations but are unable to build their own' often expressed where dangerous, hierarchical or useless organisations dominate and prevent libertarian ones being created. It can well be admitted that particular people in particular places have failed in the task of building Anarchist organisations but in many parts of the world they do exist

An organisation may be democratic or dictatorial, it may be authoritarian or libertarian, and there are many libertarian organisations, not necessarily Anarchist, which prove that all organisation need not be run from the top downwards.

Many trade unions, particularly if successful, in order to keep their movement disciplined and an integral part of capitalist society, become (if they do not start so) authoritarian; but how many employers' organisations impose similar discipline? If they do their affiliates would walk out if it did not suit their interests. They must come to free agreement because some have the means to resist intimidation. Even when they resort to fascism to keep the workers down, the employers retain their own independence and financial power; nazism goes too far for smaller capitalists in that after having crushed the workers it also limits, or even negates, the independence of the class that put it in power.

Only the most revolutionary unions of the world have ever learned how to keep the form of organisation of mass labour movements on an informal basis, with a minimum of central administration, and with every decision referred back to the workers on the shop floor. The importance of the "base" is a theme that runs through the discussions of the CNT and the IWW and remains perhaps the central problem that Anarchists have to grapple with if they are to really achieve mass support, be it in Unions or any other type of fighting organisations.

THE ROLE OF AN ANARCHIST IN AN AUTHORITARIAN SOCIETY

The only place for a free man in a slave society is in prison, said Thoreau (but he only spent a night there). It is a stirring affirmation but not one to live by. The revolutionary must be prepared for persecution and prosecution, but only the masochist would welcome it. It must always remain an individual action and decision as to how far one can be consistent in one's rebellion: it is not something that can be laid down. Anarchists have pioneered or participated in many forms of social rebellion and reconstruction, such as libertarian education, the formation of labour movements, collectivisation, individual direct action in its many forms and so on.

When we advocate anarcho-syndicalist tactics, it is

because social changes for the whole of society can only come about through a change of the economy. Individual action may serve some liberatory process, it's true. Individuals, for example, may retire to a country commune, surround themselves with like minded people and ignore the world so long as it overlooks them. They might certainly meanwhile live in a free economy if they could overcome certain basic problems, but it would not bring about social change.

This is not to decry individual action, far from it. Whole nations can live under dictatorship and sacrifice whole peoples one by one, and nobody will do anything about it until one individual comes along and cuts off the head of the hydra, in other words, kills the tyrant. But genocide can take place before the individual with the courage, ability and luck required comes along.

In such cases we see waiting for mass action as queueing up for the gas chamber (it can be literally so). We do not think "the proletariat can do no wrong" and, most of all by submission, it can. But organisation is strength. We advocate mass action because it is effective and because the proletariat has in its hands the means to destroy the old economy and build anew. The Free Society will come about through workers' councils taking over the places of work and by conscious destruction of the authoritarian structure.

They can be built within unionisation of the workforces of the present time.

Workers Control

When advocating workers control for the places of work, we differ from those who are only advocating a share of management or imagine there can be an encroachment upon managerial function by the workers within capitalism. Self-management within a capitalist society is a sizeable reform, and is occasionally attainable when the workforce is in a particularly strong position, or more often when the work is sufficiently hazardous to defy outside inspection. That is all it is, however, and is not to be confused with syndicalism, except in the sense that the syndicalist thinks the future society should be self-controlled. We want no authority supreme to that of the workers, not even one of their delegates.

This probably means breaking industry down into small units, and we accept this. We reject 'nationalisation' as a form of state control.

It should not be (but unfortunately is) necessary to explain that there are, of course, ways of personal liberation other than class action, and in some cases these may be necessary lest one starve. But none of these can at present help to change society. The self-employed artisan no longer plays an important part as in Proudhon's day (perhaps this will be revived with a new society). One can get satisfaction working on one's own, one may have to do so by economic necessity, but the means of changing society rest with those who are working in the basic economy.

Trends over recent years show the importance of the self-employed artisan. As major industries are decimated by the ruling class because they are no longer necessary to capitalism, a means of integrating those working outside mainstream capitalism will increasingly need to be found if we are to achieve change. It was the necessity of finding this in a previous reversal of capitalist trends that led to the original formation of anarcho-syndicalism.

The Anarchist as Rebel

It is not unknown for the individual Anarchist to fight on alone, putting forward his or her ideas in a hostile environment. There were many examples in the past of Anarchists struggling on alone, sometimes only one in the country. It is less the case at the present time when there are usually many people calling themselves Anarchists, though perhaps only one or two in a locality who really are so, and not just adopting the label to describe rebellion when young. Anarchists in such circumstances may fight alone for the principle of Anarchism, but usually participate in other struggles, such as anti-militarism, anti-imperialism, anti-nationalism, or solely within the context of the class struggle.

It is no part of the case for Anarchism to say that the profession of its ideas changes peoples' character; or that the movement invites itself to be judged on anyone who happened to be around at any one time. Organisations Anarchists create may become reformist or authoritarian; people themselves may become corrupted by money or power. All we can say is that ultimately such corruption normally leads them to drop the name 'Anarchist' as it stands in their way. If ever the term became 'respectable', no doubt we would have to choose a fresh one, equally connotative of libertarian rebellion – at present it can still stand as a descriptive though increasingly misused term.

In all organisations, personalities play a part and it may be that in different countries different schisms may occur. Some say that there are different types of Anarchism. Syndicalism, communism, individualism, pacifism, have all been cited as such. This is not so. If one wishes to cause a schism, purely on personal reasons or because one wishes to become more quietist or reformist, it is no doubt convenient to pick a name as a 'banner'. But in reality there are not different forms of Anarchism. Anarchist Communism, in any definition (usually that of Kropotkin) means a method of socialism without government, not a different style of Anarchism. An alternative idea, called Anarchist Collectivism, once favoured by Spanish Anarchists, was found in practice to be exactly the same. If one is going to have no rule from above, one cannot down lay down a precise economic plan for the future, and communism and collectivisation controlled from below upwards proved to be no different from each other, or from syndicalism, a permanent means of struggle towards the same goal.

Communism, in the sense used by Anarchists, is a society based on the community. Collectivism is a division of the commune into economic units. Unless the commune is very small – based upon the village – it has to be divided into smaller units, collectives, so that all can participate not just their elected representatives. Otherwise it would merely be industrial democracy. While free communism is an aim, syndicalism is a method of struggle. It is the union of workers within the industrial system attempting to transform it into a free communistic society.

State communism is not an alternative communism to free communism, but its opposite. It is the substitution of the State or the Party for the capitalist class. Communism is not necessarily Anarchist, even if it is not State Communism but the genuine authoritarian form of communism (total State control without having degenerated into absolute power from above, or even governmental dominated socialisation). Syndicalism is not necessarily revolutionary and even revolutionary syndicalism (the idea that workers can seize places of work through factory organisation) need not be libertarian, as it can go hand in hand with the idea of a political party exercising political control. This is why we use the mouthful "anarcho-syndicalism". Workers control of production, community control from below, no government from above.

Non-Violence

Is pacifism a trend within Anarchism? Though phoney Anarchism contains a large streak of pacifism, being militant liberalism and renouncing any form of positive action for Anarchism, pacifism (implying extreme non-violence, and not just anti-militarism) is authoritarian. The cult of extreme non-violence always implies an elite, the Satyagrahi of Gandhi for instance, who keep everyone else in check either by force or by moral persuasion. The general history of the orthodox pacifist movements is that they attempt to dilute a revolutionary upsurge but come down on the side of force either in an imperialist war or by condoning aggressive actions by governments they support.

Both India and Israel were once the realisation of the pacifist ideal; the atom bomb was largely developed and created by non-violent pacifists and by League of Nations enthusiasts; the Quakers as peace-loving citizens but commercial tyrants and colonialists are notorious. In recent times, many who rejected Anarchist actions of the Spanish Resistance (though claiming to be "non-violent Anarchists") had no difficulty later in supporting far more "violent" actions of different nationalist movements.

It is true to say that there are Anarchists who consider pacifism compatible with Anarchism in the sense that they advocate the use of non-violent methods though usually nowadays advocating this on the grounds of expediency or tactics rather than principle. But this should not be confused with the so-called "Tolstoyan Anarchism" (neither Tolstoyan or Anarchist). Tolstoy considered the Anarchists were right in everything but that they believed in revolution to achieve it. His idea of social change was "within one" (which is to say in the sky). He did not advocate non-violent revolution, he urged non-resistance as a way of life compatible with Christian teaching though not practised as such.

One has to say also that this refers to pacifism in the Anglo-American sense, somewhat worse in Great Britain where the concept of legalised conscientious objection led to a dialogue between pacifism and the State. In countries where objection to military service remained a totally illegal act, the concept of pacifism is not necessarily extreme non-violence.

Immediate Aims of the Anarchist

A "reformist" is not someone who brings about reforms (usually they do not, they divert attention to political manoeuvring): it is someone who can see no further than amelioration of certain parts of the system. It is necessary to agitate for the abolition of certain laws, or for the immediate reform of some, but to idealise the agitation for reforms, or even the interests in reform of minorities or even whole communities, is reformist. This reformism has permeated the whole of what is now called the left wing. It creates new industries in the interests of aspiring bureaucrats allegedly guarding over minority interests, preventing people in those minorities from acting on their own behalf. This is noticeable even in women's struggles which the left marginalises as if it were a minority issue.

Sometimes laws are more harmful than the offences they legislate against. No law is worth passing, even those which are socially beneficial on the surface, since they are sure to be interpreted wrongly, and are often used to bolster the private opinion of judges who carry them out. The old British custom of sentencing poorer classes to death for minor thefts above a small pecuniary value was not abolished by Parliament nor by the judges, but by the final refusal of juries to admit when forced to a guilty verdict that the goods were above that value.

The Anarchists can, as individuals or in groups, press for reforms but as Anarchists they seek to change minds and attitudes not to pass laws. When minds are changed, laws become obsolete and sooner or later law enforcers are unable to operate them. Prohibition in America and the Poll Tax in Britain are instances of this in action. At that point the law has to adapt itself to public opinion.

The Witchcraft Act remained on the statute books until some 40 years ago and it was enforced right up to the time of its abolition though the Public Prosecutor only dared to use a few of its clauses for fear of ridicule. It was abolished for political reasons but the equally ridiculous Blasphemy Act was retained, being unquestioned by Parliament until agitation by Muslims suggesting that it was clearly unfair that one could be fined for offending Christianity while one could not be executed for offending Islam.

The '1381' law was useful for squatters to persuade people they could occupy neglected buildings without offence, the odd thing being that the law did not exist. The myth was enough provided people believed in it.

One has to carry on a resistance to any and every form of tyranny. When governments feel their privileges are threatened, they drop the pretence of democracy and benevolence which most politicians prefer and Anarchists are forced to become what politicians describe them as: 'agents of disorder' though there is a lot more to Anarchism than that, and all 'agents of disorder' are not necessarily Anarchists.

A Marxist-Leninist would say, "Anarchists are able to bring about disorder but cannot seize power. Hence they are unable to take advantage of the situations they create, and the bourgeoisie, regrouping its strength, turns to fascism".

A Tory would say that Marxist-Leninists are Anarchists "because they wish to create Anarchy to create the conditions in which they would seize power". Both are absurdities. Anarchists can, of course, "seize power" no less than anyone just as a teetotaller can get blind drunk, but they would hardly continue to merit the name. Anarchists in power would not necessarily be any better or worse than anyone else, and they might even be as bad as communists or fascists. There is no limit of degradation to which power cannot bring anyone even with the loftiest principles. We would hope that being unprepared for power, they would be ineffective. Their task is not to "seize power" (those who use this term show that they seek personal power for themselves) but to abolish the bases of power. Power to all means power to nobody in particular.

If one leaves the wild beast of state power partially wounded, it becomes more ferocious than ever, a raging wild beast that will destroy or be destroyed. This is why Anarchists form organisations to bring about revolutionary change. The nature of Anarchism as an individualistic creed in the true sense has often caused many to say such organisations might well be left to 'spontaneity', 'voluntary will' and so on – in other words, there can be no organisation (except for propaganda only) until the entire community forms its own organisations. This is a recipe for a sort of armchair Anarchism which never gets off the ground, but at the same time, with a point that cannot be ignored – until the whole community has control of its own organisations, such bodies cannot and should not take over the social and economic means of life.

It is shown by events that unity of resistance is needed against repression, that there must be united forms of action. Even when workers' councils are formed, there may be representatives on them from political factions, united outside on party lines and able to put forward a united front within such councils and thus to dominate and ultimately destroy them. That is why we need an organised movement to destroy such efforts at totalitarianism. In some cases one may need the ultimate sanction of acts of individual terrorism to be used against leadership from within, quite as much as that imposed from above. This form of specific terrorism has nothing in common with nationalist terrorism, which by its nature is as indiscriminate as State terrorism, for all that it is judged in a far harsher light. Anarchist terrorism is against individual despots, ruling or endeavouring to rule. Nationalist terrorism is a form of war against peoples. State terrorism is the abuse of power.

Workers' Self-Defence

The Marxist-Leninists in time of revolution rely upon the formation of a Red Army. Under the control of one party, the "Red" Army is the old army under a red flag. We have seen many times how this can become a major instrument of repression, just as a Nationalist army under a new flag can also become one, sometimes even before it attains power.

The very formation of an Army to supersede workers militias will destroy the Revolution (Spain 1936). Che Guevara introduced new romantic ideas of the Red Army as the advance guard of a peasants army – combining the spontaneity of a Makhnovista

(Ukraine 1917) and Zapatista/Magonista (Mexican anarchistic) peasant army with the disciplined ideas of Party intellectuals. In such cases, after the initial enthusiasm carries it through to victory, the disciplined leadership takes over; if it fails, the leaders run off elsewhere.

The self-defence notions of anarcho-syndicalists are that workers use arms in their own defence, against the enemy at hand and that the democratic notion of workers militias prevails. While there may be technical leadership, instruction and duties such as are at present in the hands of non-commissioned officers up to the rank of sergeant, there should be no officers whose job is to command, or lower ranking NCOs to transmit the chain of command.

The idea of an armed people is derided by many so-called military and political experts, but only if used by workers in their own interests. If smaller nations use it successfully these experts admit that a citizens army – that is to say, a non-professional one that can hang up its rifles and go back to work, coming out when called upon – is possible, provided only that, as in the case of (say) Israel or South Africa, they obey nationalistic and aggressive policies from above. Providing they don't maintain the force in international class interests, the "experts" are prepared to admit the efficiency of such an army remaining democratically controlled within its own ranks.

How will a revolution come about?

We do not know. When a revolutionary situation presents itself – as it did with the occupation of factories in France 1936 and 1968; as it did in Spain 1936 with the fascist uprising; or with the breakdown of the Russian Armies 1917; or in many other times and places; we are ready for it or we are not (and usually not!!). Many times the workers are partially ready and leave the "wounded wild animal" of Statism fiercer than ever. It may be a purely individual action that sets off the spark. But only if, at that period, there is a conscious movement towards a free society that throws off the shackles of the past, will that situation become a social revolution.

The problem today that faces us is that half the world is prepared to rise almost at any opportune time, but has no military power to resist repression, and no industrial muscle to sustain itself. The other half of the world has such might, but no real desire to rise, being either bought off by capitalism or succumbing to persuasion.

BRINGING ABOUT THE NEW SOCIETY

What constitutes an Authoritarian Society?

Exploitation – Manipulation – Suppression. The organs of repression consist of many arms of the State.

The Apparatus of Government: the legislature, the judicature, the monarchy, the Civil Service, the Armed Forces, the Police etc.

The Apparatus of Persuasion: The educational system, the media, including TV, radio and the press, the Church, and even forms of apparent dissent that in reality condition us to accept the present system (the parliamentary Opposition is the most obvious, but many other alternatives to the accepted system too, e.g. revolution presented as merely one in lifestyle or musical preference, academic teaching of Marxist-Leninism etc.)

The Apparatus of Exploitation: the monetary system, financial control, the Banks, the Stock Exchange, individual, collective and State employers, land ownership. Under capitalism there is no escaping all of this.

Most political reformers have some part of the unfree system they wish to abolish. Republicans would abolish the Monarchy, Secularists would abolish or disestablish the Church; Socialists would, or used to want to, abolish the apparatus of exploitation; Pacifists would abolish the Army. Anarchism is unique in wishing to abolish all. The only true definition of an Anarchist is one who believes it is desirable to abolish all; who believes it possible to abolish all, the sooner the better; and who works to bring such abolition about.

There are many, usually on the left, who think it desirable but impossible, many on the right who think it only too probable but undesirable. Others may be sympathetic to Anarchism as both desirable and possible but refrain from action in its favour. To borrow a phrase from another part of the forest they may be fellow-travellers of Anarchism.

The police are the cornerstone of the State (though sometimes, in extreme cases, the Government of the day needs to use the armed forces in lieu of or in addition to the police – in some countries this has led to replacement or control of the government by the army so long as the officers are tightly in control).

Only Anarchism believes in abolition of the police and this is the most hotly-disputed argument of Anarchism. Yet the police force as we know it is a comparatively modern phenomenon, fiercely resisted when introduced for reasons which have since been proved up to the hilt including the ability of the police to introduce or bolster up a dictatorship, known, indeed, as a police state. Without control of the police, debates at Westminster become as sterile of result as debates in the West Kensington Debating Society (and probably less interesting).

With German money, supplied by Helphand-Parvus, Lenin was able to return to Russia and pay Lettish mercenaries to act as police. He was the only politician in a position to do so and in this way Bolshevik success was achieved. The Nazis in their turn created murder gangs that roamed the streets, which were tacitly tolerated by the Republican police, but Nazi victory came when they controlled the police by legal means.

Can One Do Without the State?

It seems to be generally agreed that we can do without some organs of the State: can we do without them all, altogether? Some are admittedly useless, some decorative, some have impossible intentions, others are necessary for class rule, some may well be useful and carry out functions essential to any society.

One cannot do the work of another. If the Monarchy has no Army it cannot save you from foreign invasion; any more than the police will get you into heaven if you do not have a church! Any commonsense codification of conduct would be better than the farrago of laws we have at present, which occupy both the lawyers and politicians, the one interpreting the apparent desires of the other.

It is true that the government can and sometimes does take over certain necessary social functions, as do every organ of the State however repressive. The railways are not always run by the State but can belong to capitalists and could equally in a future society belong to the workers. It would be foolish to say that if mines belonged to the State, that proves the State is necessary, or we would have no coal without it. The Army is often given socially necessary jobs, such as flood or earthquake relief; it is sometimes used as a scab labour force, such as in strikes; it is sometimes used as a police force. This is because the State does not want the break-up of a society that supports it.

Even the police at times fulfil some necessary functions – one goes to the police station to find lost dogs simply because it happens to be there and has taken over that function. It does not follow that we should never find lost dogs if there were no police, and that we need to be clubbed over the head in times of social unrest so that old ladies need not lose their dogs. For insurance purposes, all car owners report their lost or stolen cars to the police but it does not mean that the police force as such is indispensable.

Just as insurance companies would find some way of seeing they could not pay out on fraudulent claims, if there were no police force society would see to it that it could protect itself. Unfortunately, having a police force atrophies the ability of society to defend itself. People have lost all sense of social organisation and control. They can be put in terror by a few kids running wild, however young. The only reaction is to run to the police, and the police cannot cope.

There was an old superstition that if the Church excommunicated a country, it was under a terrible disaster. One could not be married, buried, leave property, do business in safety, be educated, be tended whilst sick, in a country that was excommunicated. The superstition was not an idle one, so long as people believed in the Church. If the country was banned from the communion of believers, the hospitals (run by the Church) were closed, there could be no trust in business (the clerics administered oaths and without them no promises need be kept), no education (they ran the schools), children could indeed be begotten (no way of preventing that by the Church!) but not christened and were therefore barred from the community of believers and under a threat, as they thought, of eternal damnation, while unmarried parents could not leave property to their "illegitimate" children. The physical reality of Hell was not necessary to make excommunication effective. We are wiser now. But one superstition has been replaced by another. It has been transferred to belief in the State. If we were to reject government there would be no education (for government, national or local controls the schools – with obvious exceptions), no hospitals (ditto), nobody could carry on working because the government regulates workplace conduct, and so on. The truth all the time has been that not the Church and not the State but we the People have worked for everything we've got, and if we have not done so they have not provided for us. Even the privileged have been maintained by us not them.

The Money Myth

With the State myth comes a second myth – the money myth. The value of money is dependent on the strength of the State. When Governments collapse, their money is worthless. For years American crooks travelled Europe offering to change Confederate dollars, worth nothing since the Southern States had lost the Civil War, presenting them to unsuspecting Europeans as valid US dollars – until they became collectors' pieces and were worth more than several US dollars! At that point the Federal Government utilised the original printing plants to publish Confederal dollars and gave them away with bubble-gum, lest their own currency became devalued.

When the Kaiser's Germany collapsed, Imperial

marks were useless. When the Spanish Republic was defeated, the banks simply cancelled the value of its money. The story is endless. Yet according to a legend many still believe, the wealth of the country is to be found at Waterlow's printing works. As the notes roll off the press, so our wealth is created, and if this ceased we should be impoverished! The banks have come up with an alternative in printing their own credit cards. Another alternative myth, now dated, was that the money printed had to correspond with a quantity of closely guarded gold buried in a mysterious vault, after having been dug up under tight security from mines thousands of miles away. However, governments have long since defaulted on the premises behind this myth (though they still continue the ritual). The newer governmental myth is that if too many notes are printed we shall have inflation which will make us all poor, so to prevent this we must be prepared to endure conditions of stringency and poverty, lose jobs and homes, or in other words become poor.

During the war, rationing of food and clothes meant that what counted was coupons, by which it was hoped to ensure there were fair shares of what was available. As the money system continued a black market in commodities was inevitable, but rationing gave an idea of what State Socialism – without money – would be like. If there were too many coupons printed there would be no point in the scheme. Money is another form of rationing, by which one set of people get more than another. Wage struggles are fights to get a bigger slice of the cake. The wealthy are those who have first access to slicing the cake. But neither money nor coupons make any difference to the size of the cake, they are simply means of dealing with its distribution, whether fairly or more likely unfairly. So essential is money to the obtaining of goods in a State society, it sounds humorous to say money is a myth – "I don't care if it's mythical, give me more" – but myth it is.

Many worthy people believe if Lady X did not spend her money on a yacht, that money could somehow be transformed into an X-ray apparatus for the hospital. They do not understand, it would seem, that yacht builders cannot produce X-ray machines. Others think that those on Unemployment Benefits are supported by those at work – yet the margin of unemployment is essential to the State as a pitfall to make the incentives to work stick. Others believe there is a relation between their wages going up and the wages received by other people going down. In a competitive society however, one gets what one is able to command.

The myth of taxation

There is a patent absurdity in supposing that those who work and produce are helped by those who profit from the system and do nothing. It is equally absurd to suppose that the rich help the poor by providing work or charity. As Brendan Behan commented to someone who pointed out how much the Guinness family had done for the poor people of Dublin – "it's nothing compared to what the poor people of Dublin have done for the Guinness family". Taxation perpetuates the myth that those with more money help those with less. Taxation grabs money out of the pockets of the less well off even before they have a chance to look at it. The rich dress up their accounts by means of professional advisors. But aside from that, money does not create wealth, it is muscle, brain and natural resources that do. Money is used to restrict the application of human endeavour. It is possible to print money, or arrange credit, when it is in the interests of money manipulators to do so. When they wish to go into recession, they do so by withdrawing money and credit. Recession is not a natural disaster like famine, drought, floods or earthquakes though it is presented as such.

The Effect of Immigration

The large scale employer looking at greater profitability or the way to cut costs has several options open, the easiest and laziest being to cut wages. If the workers are well organised they can resist this so there are two options open to the major capitalist.

Either take the factories to where the cheap labour is or take the cheap labour to where the factories are. The first option entails great pollution, as a rule – not that they ever care about that – and in some cases they have to go into areas of political instability. It is cheaper to move the cheap labour.

Having thus encouraged immigration, wearing the financial hat as it were, the capitalist in the capacity of a right-wing politician, dons the political hat and denounces immigration. This has the advantage of setting worker against worker, fuelled by religious and/or racial antipathies which can persist for generations, and have the added bonus of inducing the worker to support the right wing electorally. It does the capitalist no harm to have a work force hated by those who surround them, or in fear of deportation if they step out of line. Nor does it harm the capitalist, in a political context, to have issues such as immigration replace the basic issue of the wage and monetary system. It only becomes harmful from that point of view when a fascist force such as Hitler's gains such armed might that it can ignore the wishes of the capitalists which gave them that power and strives for its own superiority.

The Abolition of the Wage and Monetary Systems

"Socialism" has become so diffused a term today that it is used of almost any reformist or indeed positively counter-revolutionary movement that wishes to use the term and covers a multitude of ideas from liberalism to tyranny, but in reality the essentials of any socialistic theory are the abolition of the wage and monetary systems. This is because a genuine socialistic movement should be of the working class and intended for its own emancipation from wage slavery. The wage and monetary systems are the chains of that slavery that need to be broken.

Some modified form of wage or some means of exchange might be consistent with a free communistic society, especially among a post-revolutionary society accustomed to some form of labour-rewarding assessment, but the present form of monetary system is one in which money is not a servant (a means of exchange) but a boss in its own right. Wages are a means of denoting the position in society's pecking order which a person is deemed to hold. It is not even fair as regards the assessment it makes. Such systems must be swept aside.

At present, as indicated above, the Government, or the effective controller which may in some cases be over the government (the banks, for instance) assess the national wealth. A corresponding number of bank notes are printed, coin is struck, credits are granted to financial houses. According to the degree of efficiency or inefficiency of a current government (which is the stuff of day-to-day press political sloganeering and need not concern us) the assessment, or budget may be correct or incorrect. According to his or her assessment, the Chancellor of the Exchequer may be "generous" or "niggardly" in sharing out the national "cake" and apportioning our slices. But in reality salaries and wages are determined by social convention, tradition, Government patronage, economic competition, hereditary power, trade union bargaining, individual enterprise and wildcat strikes. According to their effectiveness, so is the "slice of cake" each receives. Those unable to use any of the pressures are simply left out of the reckoning and must be content with what is given them in order solely to survive. The "cake" is the same whatever the Government does about it.

Is Anarchism compatible with Capitalism?

It is only possible to conceive of Anarchism in a form in which it is free, communistic and offering no economic necessity for repression or countering it. Commonsense shows that any capitalist society might dispense with a "State" (in the American sense of the word) but it could not dispense with organised government, or a privatised form of it, if there were people amassing money and others working to amass it for them. The philosophy of "anarcho-capitalism" dreamed up by the "libertarian" New Right, has nothing to do with Anarchism as known by the Anarchist movement proper. It is a lie that covers an unple-

53

asant reality in its way – such as National Socialism does in another. Patently unbridled capitalism, not even hampered by a reformist State, which has to put some limits on exploitation to prevent violent clashes in society, needs some force at its disposal to maintain class privileges, either from the State itself or from private armies. What they believe in is in fact a limited State – that is, one in which the State has one function, to protect the ruling class, does not interfere with exploitation, and comes as cheap as possible for the ruling class. The idea also serves another purpose beyond its fulfilment – a moral justification for bourgeois consciences in avoiding taxes without feeling guilty about it – just as pacifism sometimes serves as an excuse for bourgeois consciences in avoiding danger without feeling guilty.

Community Control

The history of collective control in a capitalist society is a pretty dismal one. There have been many attempts to bypass the system by forming "communities" which because they are less than the whole, real community, are bound in the end not to prosper. Co-operative societies no less than small businesses rarely withstand the pressure of monopoly capitalism. Collective farms, collective enterprises at which one works at less than the normal wage to for the sake of independence, like craft businesses, never quite get off the ground and it always comes down to the monopoly market. All could flourish if the system were free, but it is not.

Nevertheless, one can note that many communal products are equally available to all, either on payment of a fixed sum, or free. The highways are free – neither State nor capitalism has got round (yet) to making all roads toll roads to enter which one must pay (but they've got round to it on main motorways on the Continent). It would probably make no economic difference if the underground railway was also free, bearing in mind the cost of ticket collecting. Water used to be free – even when water rates came in one could draw as much as one liked from the tap. Now there are water meters, as if we were living in the Sahara where water has long been rationed. So far they have not got round to making us pay for air.

Anarchism presupposes that all these arguments based on economics are bunkum. Services which come naturally or are produced by the people should belong to the people.

Need there be a Transitional Society?

A transitional society to Anarchism isn't necessary. The idea touted by Leninists was that the State would fade away after years of the harshest dictatorship

– originally claimed to be only as much as was necessary to save the infant Soviet Republic but which lasted for seventy years until the people got fed up with it. All that faded away was people rash enough to want to go forward to free socialism. The prospect of 'withering away of the State' after years of strengthening it is illogical. Leninists justify this by saying the State is only that part of the State apparatus which favours the capitalist class by suppressing the working class. This might fade away (though it did not do so in the years of State Communism). What cannot fade away is the rest of the State apparatus, unless the State is destroyed root and branch.

The fact that a transitional society to Anarchism isn't necessary does not necessarily mean there will not be one. Who can say? After all, changing attitudes to such matters as racial domination, sexual discrimination, religious orientation, conformity, and so on might be part of a transition to a free society already existing. There might be an occupation of the places of work without a conscious revolution, which in itself would be a transitional period.

One could even visualise a curious transitional period in which part of society was evolving to a new system and part was sticking to the old – with workers control co-existing with private capitalism in the market the way rigid old-time family styles co-exist with free relationships in the same street. But

56

clearly in the long run one or the other system would have to go. Capitalism could not exist if people could be free to choose the way they work without being compelled by conscription or necessity – therefore it would either need to reinforce its authority (possibly by fascist gangs, as during the occupation of the factories in Italy) or go under (which is the choice the Italian capitalists as a whole were forced to take, even though many subscribed to democracy, emotionally or politically.)

A Free Society

A society cannot be free unless not only are there no governmental restraints, but the essentials of life are free in that sense too.

It is true that if some products were in short supply, however free the society access to them would have to be rationed by some means. It could be by 'labour value' cards, by ordinary 'fair rationing', it might imply retention of a different monetary system (but not money as an end in itself, in which money has a value beyond that of exchanging goods).

We cannot lay down the economics for a free society which by its nature is free to reject or accept anything it fancies. The authoritarian economist can do so ("so long as I, or my party, is in power, we will do

57

this or that"). Some Anarchist economists like Isaac Puente have worked on creating guidelines for achieving Anarchism. These guidelines, though, are suggestions rather than recipes.

An Anarchist society is by definition a free society, but a free society is not necessarily Anarchist. It might fall short in several respects. Some failings might seriously limit its desirability. For instance, a revolution carried out by men in a male-dominated society, might perpetuate sex discrimination which would limit freedom and undermine the revolution by leaving it possible for aggressive attitudes to be fostered. The liberal illusion that repressive forces must be tolerated which will ultimately wipe out all freedom, lest the right to dissent be imperilled, could well destroy the revolution.

A free society needs to rid itself of repressive institutions and some might last longer than others. The Church is one instance – yet religious beliefs, which continue under the most repressive and brutal dictatorships, could surely continue under No Government. Only those creeds which have not had their claws cut and demand suppression of other religions or unbelief, forced conversions or marriages, censorship by themselves and obedience to their own laws from those not wishing to do so, have anything to fear from an Anarchist Revolution. Anarchists will often come back to Spain as these ideas were debated by the Spanish Anarchists when Anarchism looked possible. Their ideas and practices are essential reading, covering areas such as sexual politics, morality, vegetarianism and the implications of the class struggle and individual freedom. Only now as more and more documentation comes to light are we able to appreciate the sophistication of these debates sixty years ago.

The Employers Do Not Give Work

It is basic socialist thinking, to which Anarchism subscribes, that work is not something that is given by the employer. The employer may have the legal right to distribute work, but the wealth of a country is due to the workers and to natural resources, not to an employer or a State.

It is the Anarchist case that fluctuations of the money market, inflation, recession, unemployment, as well as war, are artificially created and are not natural disasters like flood, famine, earthquake, drought – and as one knows nowadays, even some of these are created by abuse of natural resources.

It may be that in some technological society of the future, run by the State, in a sort of boss utopia, the working class will be displaced as a productive class. We see signs of that even today as large parts of the economy are closed down as unprofitable and people uprooted. There is a technology, still in its infancy but making great strides, which will reduce us, as a productive class, to turners of switches and openers of the scientists' doors; to secretaries and receptionists; to janitors and clerks; to domestic servants of the rich. Anarcho-syndicalists think such a society must be resisted. They do not worship work as a fetish in itself but fight dehumanisation and alienation. In this they differ from some other Anarchists who think work has no purpose and who become state-dependent by conviction.

OBJECTIONS TO ANARCHISM

Whenever Anarchists attack present-day society, they touch on the fears and prejudices of average people who know that society is a jungle today and cannot visualise life without the safeguards needed in the jungle. When they hear of Anarchism they bring forward objections which are, in fact, criticisms of the present system rather than criticisms of the free society of the future.

They fear what is known in the Statist language as a "state of anarchy" – they think murder, rape, robbery, violent attack would ensue if there were no government to prevent it. And yet we all know that government cannot, certainly does not, prevent these evils. One has only to pick up the papers to learn that they flourish though government is strong, and also where government is weak, and more so perhaps where there are numerous bodies competing as to which is the real government and where government is said to have broken down. A "state of anarchy" nowhere exists – in the sense of a society where there is no government and not just a weak or divided government.

The most a functioning government can do is not prevent but punish – when it finds out, sometimes wrongly or not at all – who the culprits are. Its own methods of repressive action can cause far more damage than the original crimes – the "cure" is worse than the disease.

"What would you do without a police force?" Anarchists are always asked. Society would never tolerate murder, whether it had a police force or not. The institutionalisation of a body to look after crime means that it not only "looks after" and nourishes crime, but that the rest of society is absolved from doing so. The reasoning is that a murder next door is the State's business, not mine! Responsibility for one's neighbour is reduced in an authoritarian society, in which the State is solely responsible for our behaviour.

"Who will do the dirty work?". This is a question society, not just the apologist for Anarchism, has to ask itself. There are dirty jobs which are socially unacceptable and poorly paid, so that nobody wants to do them. People have therefore been enslaved to do them, or there is competition in a market economy and the jobs become better paid (and therefore socially acceptable), or there is conscription for such jobs, whether by political direction or the pressures of unemployment. Sometimes the capitalist introduces immigration in the hope of cheap labour, thus putting off the problem for a generation or two. Or it can be the jobs don't get done and, say, the streets aren't swept any more and so we get deluged with water shooting out from cars driven by graduate psychologists and step gingerly past refuse, clutching our theses on sociological impulses.

What the State does in such circumstances seems to depend on political factors. What an Anarchist society would do could only be foretold by a clairvoyant. It is plain what it could not do – use force, since it would lack repressive machinery or the means of economic coercion. Again we must look back to History. Barcelona 1936, Hungary 1956, countless other less documented sources where people have taken control of their lives into their own hands.

"If the Anarchists do not seize power, and have superseded other forms of socialism that would, they objectively make way for fascism". This allegation presupposes the dilution of Anarchism with pacifism, for there is always, in any circumstances, one sure way of avoiding dictatorship, whether from the right, left, centre or within one's own ranks, and that is by personal removal of the dictator. This only becomes a symbolic gesture when the dictator is in power with all the machinery of command-and-obey at the disposal of the head of State.

Anyone will seize power if given the opportunity. Anarchists do not claim to be a privileged elite and cannot truthfully assert they would be better able to resist the temptations of power, or to wield it more successfully, than anyone else.

Leadership

Do Anarchists believe in leadership? They always deny they do, but undoubtedly many Anarchists have emerged as leaders, sometimes even of armies (like Buenaventura Durruti, Cipriano Mera and Nestor Makhno) or of ideas, or of organisations. In any grouping some people do naturally "give a lead", but this should not mean they are a class apart. What they always reject is institutionalised leadership. That means their supporters become blind followers and the leadership not one of example or originality but of unthinking acceptance.

Musical geniuses, artists, scientists can be of an "elite" without being elitist – there is no reason why excelling in certain spheres should make one better entitled to the world's goods or more worthy of consideration in matters in which one does not have specialised knowledge (the correspondence between Freud and Einstein in which they discuss whether war can be prevented is a classic example of futility – Einstein looking to Freud for a psychological lead in pacifism and Freud explaining it is in the nature of Man. In the end scientists who were pacifists or believers in the League of Nations or, like Einstein both, invented the atom bomb).

In the same way, people can work in an office without being bureaucrats: a bureaucrat is a person whose power is derived from the office they hold. In slang it is a term flung at anyone who happens to be efficient, which is far from being the same thing.

In the same way no real Anarchist, as distinct from someone pretending to be one, would agree to be part of an *institutionalised leadership*. Neither would an Anarchist wait for a lead, but give one. That is the mark of being an Anarchist, not a formal declaration of being one. What above all is the curse of leadership is not the leaders themselves, but agreement to being led blindly – not the faults of the shepherd but the meekness of the sheep. What would the crimes of Hitler have amounted to, had he had to carry them out by himself?

Can Public Opinion Itself be Authoritarian?

Yes. Even in a free society? Certainly. But this is not an argument against a free society, it is a reason why public opinion should not be moulded by an outside force. There might well be a society controlled economically by the workers where prejudice against some minorities, or traditional family attitudes, or rules laid down by religions rooted in the past, might still exist. The society would be free in one respect only, economically.

But without any means of codifying prejudices, no repressive machinery against nonconformists, above all no means of repression by persuasion when the media is controlled from above, public opinion can become superior to its prejudices. The majority is not automatically right. The manipulation of the idea of a majority is part of the government technique.

Unity

One last objection is made against Anarchism, usually by those about to "come over" – Why disunity in the ranks of those who take up a similar position on many stands? Why cannot we be all one libertarian left? Why any divisions at all?

If we create councils of action – workers' industrial proto-unions – as we intend to do given the chance and agreement of workers, even if as a first step we form social groups based upon industrial activity or support, obviously we are going to be united to others not only of the libertarian left, but also (in the case of workers' councils) with people of reformist, reactionary or authoritarian points of view. We mix with them in everyday life anyway. The expression of Anarchist views and attitudes does not make us hermits. Anarchist groups need to keep alive their identity, but only a party machine would make them into walls preventing meeting others outside them.

It is certainly the curse of the present day that pseudo-Anarchists, whether liberal or "lifestylist" create their own ghettos within a left, which has become itself a ghetto, in which acceptance of a package deal of ideas is obligatory. This endemic isolation, in the name of youth, sex, race, nationality, alternative culture, punk or whatever, has nothing to do with Anarchism though it has been wished on it by journalistic propaganda and encouraged by those who mistake packaging for practical substance. Anarchism is not a form of dress or a liking for a certain type of music. It is not the discussion of ideas in the pub or other social setting. Neither is it, necessarily, membership of some or other Anarchist group. It is practical activity which in whatever small way helps to increase mutual aid, destroy capitalism and bring about libertarian communism. It is activity that opens out, rather than closes down into the dead end of political elitism. As for libertarian communism … well… as Isaac Puente wrote "Libertarian Communism will be like learning to live".

THE MARXIST CRITICISM OF ANARCHISM

The Marxist criticism of Anarchism is the first with which most people with a serious interest in politics come in contact. There follows from it the Marxist-Leninist critique and the Social-Democratic objections.

Marxist-Leninists, faced with Anarchism, find that by its nature it undermines all the suppositions basic to Marxism. Marxism was held out to be the basic working class philosophy (a belief which has utterly ruined the working class movement everywhere). It holds in theory that the industrial proletariat cannot owe its emancipation to anyone but themselves alone. It is hard to go back on that and say that the working class is not yet ready to dispense with authority placed over it by someone outside the class.

Marxism normally tries to refrain from criticising

Anarchism as such – unless driven to doing so, when it exposes its own authoritarianism ("how can the workers run the railways, for instance, without direction – that is to say, without authority?") and concentrates its attack not on Anarchism, but on Anarchists. This is based on a double standard: Anarchists are held responsible for the thought and actions of all persons, live or dead, calling themselves Anarchists (even only temporarily) or persons referred to as Anarchists by others even on a faulty premise! Marxists take responsibility only for Marxists holding their particular party card at the time.

Marxism has – whether one agrees with it or not – a valid criticism of the Anarchists in asking how one can (now) dispense with political action – or whether one should throw away so vital a weapon. But this criticism varies between the schools of Marxism, since some have used it to justify complete participation in the whole capitalist power structure, whilst others talk vaguely only of "using parliament as a platform". Lenin recognised the shortcomings of Marxism in this respect and insisted that the Anarchist workers could not be criticised for rejecting so Philistine a Marxism that it used political participation for its own sake and expected the capitalist state to let itself be voted out of existence peacefully. He therefore concentrated on another aspect, which Marx pioneered, viz. criticism of particular Anarchists; and this has dominated all Leninist thinking ever since.

Because of the lack of any other criticism of the Anarchists, Leninists – especially Trotskyists – to this day use the personal criticism method. But as Lenin selected only a few well known personalities who for a few years fell short of the ideas they preached, the latter-day Leninists have to hold that all Anarchists are responsible for every one who calls himself or herself an Anarchist – or even (such as the Russian Socialist-Revolutionaries in Russia) were only called such by others.

This wrinkle in Leninism has produced another criticism of Anarchism (usually confined to Trots and Maoists); Anarchists are responsible not only for everyone referred to as Anarchists, but for all workers influenced by Anarchist ideas. The C.N.T. is always quoted here, but significantly its whole history before and after the civil war is never mentioned, solely the period of participation in the government. For this, the Anarchists must for ever accept responsibility! But the Trots may back the reformist union U.G.T. without accepting any compromising or treacherous period in its entire history. In all countries (if workers) they presumably join or (if students) accept, the reformist trade unions. That is all right. But a revolutionary trade union must for ever be condemned for any one deviation. Moreover, if broken it must never be rebuilt; the reformist union must be rebuilt in preference. This is the logical consequence of all Trot thinking on Spain or other countries where such unions exist, proving their preference for the negative character of reformist unions which lends itself to a leadership they may capture; as against a decentralised union which a leadership cannot capture.

Petty Bourgeois

Not withstanding this preference for non-revolutionary unions, and condemnation of Anarchists for unions built from the bottom up, all Marxist-Leninists have a seemingly contradictory criticism of Anarchists, namely "they are petty bourgeois".

This leads them into another difficulty: how can one reconcile the existence of anarcho-syndicalist unions with "petty bourgeois" origins – and how does one get over the fact that most Marxist-Leninists of today are professional ladies and gentlemen studying for, or belonging to, the conservative professions? The answer is usually given that because Anarchism is "petty bourgeois" those embracing it, "whatever their occupation or social origins", must also be "petty bourgeois"; and because Marxism is working class, its adherents must be working class "at least subjectively". This is a sociological absurdity, as if "working class" meant an ideological viewpoint. It is also a built-in escape clause.

Yet Marx was not such a fool as his followers. "Petty bourgeois" in his day did not mean a solicitor or an accountant, a factory manager, sociologist or anything of that sort. They were "bourgeois" – the term was "petit" (small) not "petty" that qualified the adjective – and meant precisely that these were not the same as bourgeoisie. The small burgher was one who had less privileges, economically, than the wealthy, but had some privileges by virtue of his craft. Anarchism, said Marx, was the movement of the artisan worker – that is to say, the self-employed craftsman with some leisure to think and talk, not subject to factory hours and discipline, independently minded and difficult to threaten, not backward like the peasantry. In England, these people tended to become Radicals, perhaps because the State was less oppressive and less obviously unnecessary. In many countries, however, they were much more extreme in their radicalism and in the Swiss Jura the clockmakers' Anarchism prospered. It spread to Paris – and the Paris Commune was above all a rising of the artisans who had been reduced to penury by Napoleon III and his war. As the capitalist structure spread throughout the world, the artisans were ruined and driven into the factories. It is these individual craftsmen entering industrialisation who became Anarchists, pointed out successive Marxists. They were not conditioned to factory discipline which produces good order unlike a proletariat prepared to accept a leadership and a party, and to work for ever in the factory provided it comes under State control.

That this observation was true is seen by the crushing of the Commune in Paris and the workers movement in Spain and throughout the world, especially in places like Italy, Bulgaria, in the Jewish pale of settlement in Russia, and so on. It should be the task of an Anarchist union movement to seize the factories, but only in order to break down mass production and get back to craftsmanship. This is what Marx meant by a "petit bourgeois" outlook and the term having changed its meaning totally, the Marxists, like believers accepting Holy Writ, misunderstood him totally.

Vanguards

The reluctance of Marxist-Leninists to accept change is, however, above all seen in the acceptance of Lenin's conception of the Party (It is not that of Marx). Lenin saw that Russia was a huge mass of inertia, with a peasantry that would not budge but took all its suffering with "Asiatic" patience. He looked to the "proletariat" to push it. But the "proletariat" was only a small part of the Russia of his day. Still he recognised it as the one class with an interest in progress – provided, he felt, it was led by shrewd, calculating, ruthless and highly educated people (who could only come from the upper classes in the Russia of the time). The party they created should become, as much as possible, the party of the proletariat in which that class could organise and seize power. It had then the right and the duty to wipe out all other parties.

The idiocy of applying this today, in say a country like Britain, is incredible. One has only to look at the parties which offer themselves as the various parties of the proletariat, of which, incidentally, there could be only one. Compare them with the people around. The parties' membership are far behind ordinary people in political intelligence and understanding. They are largely composed of shallow and inexperienced, enthusiasts who understand far less about class struggle than the average worker.

Having translated the Russian Revolution into a mythology which places great stress on the qualities possessed by its leadership, they then pretend to possess that leadership charisma. But they don't have it. There is a total divorce between the working class and the so-called New Left, which has therefore to cover itself up with long-winded phrases in the hope that this will pass for learning. In the wider "Movement", with the definitions at second hand from Marxist-Leninism, they scratch around to find someone really as backward and dispossessed as the moujik, and fall back on the "Third World" mythology.

The one criticism applied by Marxist-Leninists of Anarchism with any serious claim to be considered is, therefore, solely that of whether political action should be considered or not. Whenever it has been undertaken it has proved of benefit only to leaders from outside the class.

THE SOCIAL-DEMOCRATIC CRITIQUE OF ANARCHISM

The early socialists did not understand that there would be necessarily a difference between Anarchism and socialism. Both were socialist, but whereas the latter hoped to achieve socialism by parliamentary means, the former felt that revolutionary means were necessary. As a result many early Anarchist and socialist groups (especially in Britain) were interchangeable in working class membership. Something might come from political action; something by industrial methods. The revolution had to be fought as soon as possible; the one therefore was complementary to the other though it was recognised that they might have to follow separate paths.

This, however, changed because the face of socialism changed. It dropped its libertarian ideas for Statism. "Socialism" gradually came to mean State Control of everything and therefore, so far from being another face of Anarchism, was its direct opposite. From saying originally that "the Anarchists were too impatient" the parliamentary socialists turned to a criticism of the Anarchists levelled at them by people who had no desire to change society at all, whether sooner or later. They picked up what is essentially the conservative criticism of Anarchism which is that the State is the arbiter of all legality and the present economic order is the only established legal order. A stateless society – or even its advocacy – is thus regarded as criminal in itself! It is not as a law but to this day a police constable in court – or a journalist – will, for this reason, refer to Anarchism as if it were self-evidently criminal.

Most upholders of any parliamentary system deliberately confuse parliamentarism with democracy as an ideal system of equal representation, as if it already existed. Thus ultra-parliamentarism is "undemocratic", suggesting that a few hundred men and a few dozen women selected at random and alone had the right of exercising control over the rest of the country.

Since the Russianisation of "Communism", turning away from both parliamentarism and democracy, it has suited the social-democrat to speak of criticism from the revolutionary side as being necessarily from those wanting dictatorship. The Anarchists, who can hardly be accused of dictatorship – except by politically illiterate journalists who do not understand the differences between parties – must therefore be "criminal" and whole labour movements have been so stigmatised by the Second International. This was picked up by the U.S. Government with its "criminal syndicalism" legislation which was similar to that in more openly fascist countries.

No more than the Marxist-Leninists, the Social-Democrats (in the sense of orthodox Labourites) are unable to state that their real objection to Anarchism is the fact that it is against power and privilege and so undermines their whole case. They bring up, if challenged, the objection that it is "impossible". If "impossible", what have they to fear from it? Why, in countries like Spain and Portugal, where the only chance of resisting tyranny was the Anarchist Movement, did Social-Democrats prefer to help the Communist Party? In post-war Spain up to the appearance of the Socialist Party when it was politically profitable to switch, the British Labour Party helped the Communist-led factions but did nothing for the Anarchist resistance.

Dictatorship of the proletariat is "possible" – only too much so. When it comes it will sweep the socialists away. But if the Anarchists resist, the socialists will at least survive to put forward their alternative. They fear only the consequences of that alternative being decisively rejected – for who would choose State Socialism out of the ashcan for nothing if they could have Stateless Socialism instead?

In the capitalist world, the social democrat objects to revolutionary methods, the "impatient" and alleged "criminality" of the Anarchists. But in the communist world, social democracy was by the same conservative token equally "criminal", indeed more so, since it presumably postulated connection with enemy powers, as is now proved. The charge of "impatience" could hardly be levelled when there was no way of effecting a change legally and the whole idea of change by parliamentary methods was a dream. Social-Democracy, in the sense of Labourism, gives up the fight without hope when tyranny triumphs (unless it can call on foreign intervention, as in Occupied war-time Europe). It has nothing to offer. There is no struggle against Fascism or Leninism from Social-Democracy because no constitutional methods offer themselves. In the former Soviet Union and its satellites they had no ideas on how to change and hoped that nationalists and religious dissidents would put through a bit of liberalism to ease the pressure. We know now how disastrous that policy has been. Yet Anarchism offers a revolutionary attack upon the communist countries that is not only rejected by the social-democrats. They actually unite with other capitalist powers to harass and suppress that attack.

THE LIBERAL-DEMOCRATIC OBJECTION TO ANARCHISM

Liberal-Democracy, or non-fascist conservatism, is afraid to make direct criticisms of Anarchism because to do so undermines the whole reasoning of liberal-democracy. It therefore resorts to falsification: Anarchists are equated with Marxists (and thereby the whole Marxist criticism of Anarchism ignored). The most frequent target of attack is to suggest that Anarchism is some form of Marxism plus violence, or some extreme form of Marxism.

The reason liberal-democracy has no defence to offer against real Anarchist argument is because liberal-democracy is using it as its apologia in the defence of "freedom" yet placing circumscribing walls around it. It pretends that parliamentarism is some form of democracy, but though sometimes prepared to admit (under pressure) that parliamentarism is no form of democracy at all, occasionally seeks to find ways of further democratising it. The undoubtedly dictatorial process that a few people, once elected, by fair means or foul, have a right to make decisions for a majority, is covered up by a defence of the Constitutional Rights or even the individual liberty of Members of Parliament. Burke's dictum that they are representatives, not delegates, is quoted ad nauseam as if this reactionary politician had bound the British people for ever, though he, as he himself admitted, did not seek to ask their opinions of the matter once.

Liberal economics are almost as dead as the dodo. What rules is either the monopoly of the big firms, or of the State. Yet laissez-faire economics remain embodied in the aspirations of the Tory Party. They object to the intervention of the State in business, but they never care to carry the spirit of competition too far. There is no logical reason why there should be any restriction on the movement of currency – and this is good Tory policy (though never implemented! Not until the crisis, any crisis, is over!). From this point of view, why should we not be able to deal in gold pieces or U.S. dollars or Maria Theresa tales or Francs or Deutschmarks or even devalued Deutschmarks? The pound sterling would soon find its own level, and if it were devalued, so much the worse for it. But why stop there? If we can choose any currency we like free socialism could co-exist with capitalism and it would drive capitalism out.

Once free socialism competes with capitalism – as it would if we would choose to ignore the State's symbolic money and deal in one of our own choosing which reflected real work values – who would choose to be exploited? Quite clearly no laissez-faire economist who had to combine his role with that of party politician would allow things to go that far.

Liberal-Democracy picks up one of the normal arguments against Anarchism which begin on the right wing; namely it begins with the objections against socialism – that is statism – but if there is an anti-statist socialism that is in fact more liberal than itself, then it is "criminal". If it is not, then it seeks law to make it so.

This argument is in fact beneath contempt, yet it is one that influences the press, police and judiciary to a surprising extent. In fact Anarchism as such (as distinct from specific Anarchist organisations) could never be illegal, because no laws can make people love the State. It is only done by false ideals such as describing the State as "country".

The fact is that liberal-democracy seldom voices any arguments against Anarchism as such – other than relying on prejudice – because its objections are purely authoritarian, and unmask the innate Statism and authoritarianism of liberalism. Nowadays conservatives like to appropriate the name "liberalism" to describe themselves as if they were more receptive to freedom than socialists. But their liberalism is confined to keeping the State out of interfering in their business affairs. Once Anarchism makes it plain that it is possible to have both social justice and to dispense with the State they are shown in their true colours. Their arguments against State Socialism and Communism may sound "libertarian", but

80

their arguments against Anarchism reveal that they are essentially authoritarian. That is why they prefer to rely upon innuendo, slanders and false reporting, which is part of the Establishment's anti-Anarchism, faithfully supported by the media.

THE FASCIST OBJECTION TO ANARCHISM

The fascist objection to Anarchism is, curiously enough, more honest than that of the Marxist, the Liberal or the Social-Democrat. Most of these will say, if pressed, that Anarchism is an ideal, perhaps imperfectly understood, but either impossible of achievement or possible only in the distant future. The Fascist, on the contrary, admits its possibility. What is denied is its desirability.

The right wing authoritarian (which term includes many beyond those naming themselves fascists) worships the very things which are anathema to Anarchists, especially the State. Though the conception of the State is idealised in fascist theory, it is not denied that one could do without it. But the "first duty of the citizen is to defend the State" and it is high treason to oppose it or advocate its abolition.

Sometimes the State is disguised as the "corporate people" or the "nation" giving a mystical idea of the State beyond the mere bureaucratic apparatus of rule. The forces of militarism and oppression are idealised (after the German Emperor who said that universal peace was "only a dream and not even a good dream"). Running throughout right wing patriotism is a mystical feeling about the "country", but, though Nazis in particular sometimes have recourse to an idealisation of the "people" (this has more of a racial than popular connotation in German) it is really the actual soil that is held sacred, thus taking the State myth to its logical conclusion. For the Anarchist this, of course, is nonsense. The nonsense can be seen in its starkest form with the followers of Franco who killed off so many Spaniards even after the civil war was ended, while hankering for the barren rock of Gibraltar.

Anarchism is clearly seen by Fascists as a direct menace and not a purely philosophical one. It is not merely the direct action of Anarchists but the thing itself which represents the evil. The "democratic" media finally got round to picking up these strands in fascist thinking, ironing them out nicely, and presenting them in the "news" stories. Hitler regarded the authoritarian state he had built as millennial (the thousand year state) but he knew it could be dismembered and rejected. His constant theme was the danger of this and while he concentrated (for political reasons) attacks on a totalitarian rival, State Communism (since Russia presented a military menace), his attacks on "cosmopolitanism" have the reiterated theme of anti-Anarchism.

"Cosmopolitanism" and "Statelessness" are the "crimes" Nazism associated with Jews though since Hitler's day large numbers of them have reverted to nationalism and a strong state. The theme of "Jewish domination" goes hand in hand with "Anarchist destruction of authority, morals and discipline", since fascism regards personal freedom as bad in itself and only national freedom permissible. Insofar as one can make any sense of Hitler's speeches (which are sometimes deceptive since he followed different strands of thought according to the way he could sway an audience), he believed the "plunging into Anarchy" of a country (abolition of State restraints) will lead to chaos, which will make it possible for a dictatorship, other than the one in the people's interests, to succeed.

Hitler did not confuse State Communism with Anarchism, as Franco did deliberately for propaganda purposes in order to try and eradicate Anarchism from history. He equated communism with "Jewish domination" and the case against the Jews (in original Nazi thinking) was that they are a racially pure people who will gain conquest over helots like the Germans. A "Master Race" must control the Germans to keep the rival State out. In a condition of freedom the German "helots" would revert to anarchy, just as the racially "inferior" Celts of France threw out the Norman Nordic overlords (the Houston Chamberlain version of the French Revolution). Later, of course, when Nazism became a mass party it was expedient to amend this to saying the Germans were the Master Race, but this was not the original Nazi philosophy nor was it privately accepted by the Nazi leaders ("the German people were not worthy of me"). But they could hardly tell mass meetings that they were all "helots". At least not until their power was complete. This idea that a whole people (whichever it was) can be born "helots" could not be better expressed as the contrary opposite of Anarchism, since in this case it would indeed be impossible.

This Nazi propaganda is echoed by the media today; "plunging the country into Anarchy would be followed by a Communist or extreme right-wing dictatorship" is current newspaper jargon.

To sum up the fascist objection to Anarchism: it is not denied the abolition of the State can come about, but if so, given economic, social and political freedom, the "helots" – who are "naturally inclined" to accept subjection from superior races – will seek for masters. They will have a nostalgia for "strong rule".

In Nazi thinking, strong rule can only come from (in theory) racially pure members of the "Master Race" (something a little more than a class and less than a people), which can be constructive masters (i.e. the "Aryans"), or a race which has had no contact with the "soil" and will be thus destructive.

In other types of Fascist thinking, given freedom, the people will throw off all patriotic and nationalistic allegiances and so the "country" will cease to be great. This is the basis of Mussolini's fascism, and of course, it is perfectly true, bearing in mind that "the country" is his synonym for the State and his only conception of greatness is militaristic. The frankest of all is the Spanish type of fascism which sought to impose class domination of the most brutal kind and make it plain that its opposition to Anarchism was simply in order to keep the working class down. If necessary, the working class may be, and was, decimated in order to crush Anarchism.

It is true of all political philosophies, and blatant with the fascist one, that its relationship to Anarchism throws a clear light upon itself!

TRADE UNION (AND ANTI-TRADE UNION) OBJECTIONS TO ANARCHISM

Trade unionists often regard anarcho-syndicalism as a direct menace, sometimes viewing the Anarchist objections to authoritarian leadership and to the closed shop as equivalent with Conservative attacks on free trade unionism. Yet at the same time Conservatives view anarcho-syndicalism as 'trade unionism gone mad.' (One Spanish Rightist said the CNT consisted of 'bandits with union cards' – and in a situationist-like phrase another said 'the crime of industrialisation led to the industrialisation of crime.')

But some package-deal libertarians think anarcho-syndicalism is just another form of trade unionism and their objections are based on their repulsions to trade unionism, or even work as such.

What's the difference between the two? Both derive directly from the idea of workers' co-operation.

TRADE UNIONISM is an association of workers for the betterment of their conditions. While its pressures for wages and job security cause it to form political alliances, these differ from country to country. In the USA union leaders tend to make deals with the capitalists, often for the immediate cash and security advantages of their members, sometimes for the leadership; in this country union leaders have formed the Labour Party, are less inclined to deal with capitalism, or nationalism.

ANARCHO-SYNDICALISM which does not differ

from country to country except in the degree to which workers find it applicable to their immediate needs and interests, is concerned with the taking over of industry by the workers and therefore supersedes any political alliance; it does seek, by direct action, to improve pay and job security, but its main aim is revolutionary change and workers control.

TRADE UNIONISM tends to become a division of the working class separating employed from unemployed/unwaged, and creating job categories to which one is very often bound for life. It is sometimes, in the English system certainly, impossible to get a job unless you have a union card and impossible to get a union card unless you have a job.

ANARCHO-SYNDICALISM is based on the unity of all the workers in the region, grouping all employed, unemployed or self-employed in the local workers' centre, and providing entry regardless of 'category.'

TRADE UNIONISM in many countries looks to a closed shop to defend the workers' interests, which – while it means on the one hand the union can obtain limited reforms or increases for all – also means the union is dependent more on parliamentary action than industrial action. The leadership becomes all-powerful since once it exerts its right to expel a member, that person is not only out of the union, but out of a job.

ANARCHO-SYNDICALISM rejects the closed shop and relies on voluntary membership, and so avoids any leadership or bureaucracy. One or two paid officials suffice for a membership of thousands, and sometimes even that much is considered unnecessary.

TRADE UNIONISM is generally for State intervention, unless it is (as in the USA or West Germany) entirely sold on private enterprise. Its highest aim is to influence or control the State.

ANARCHO-SYNDICALISM fights private enterprise and State control alike. Its aim is to abolish both.

On the whole workers prefer Trade Unionism when it is delivering the goods in the form of cash payments and job security; and so long as they can criticise its shortcomings, they fatally accept that its leadership is fairly immovable and inevitably bound to considerations other than the welfare of their members.

The workers prefer Anarcho-syndicalism when they need a tough union, and when they are imbued with libertarian ideas as against accepting authoritarian ideas or taking their ideas from the media.

The term 'Syndicalist' – as distinct from Anarcho-syndicalist – has three or four meanings in organised labour. In Italy, France and Spain it is simply an interchangeable term for trade unionist. In the English-speaking countries, where the term trade unionist is normal language, syndicalism has been taken to mean revolutionary trade unionism, in other words trade unions working towards social change, not necessarily Anarchist. Sometimes it has been used interchangeably with Anarcho-syndicalist, or used as a euphemism for the latter when Anarcho- tends to scare. It has also been used to mean militant – as distinct from revolutionary – trade unionism, aiming at control, not directly by the working class, but by the leadership in particular of the trade unions themselves.

There can no doubt be forms of Anarchism which reject Syndicalism, which normally means they reject the whole idea of class struggle, and logically any form of activity other than protesting about the iniquities of the State system, without any intention of changing it: this is militant liberalism or mere permanent protest, masquerading as Anarchism.

The term Council Communism is almost synonymous with Anarcho-syndicalism in its original German usage: with the exception that Anarcho-syndicalism is the most militant expression of working class activity imbued with Anarchist ideas, and Council Communism the most militant, and libertarian, expression of a working class imbued with Marxist ideas (but not Bolshevik/Leninist ones: this is the anti-thesis of Council communism) coming to similar conclusions by a different road. However, the prevalent modern usage of the term Council Communism in 'Situationist'-type circles is by those who reject Anarcho-syndicalism because it believes in a permanent organisation of workers. They want the workers to organise 'spontaneously' at the very moment of revolution. This is a con-trick, designed to leave 'the revolutionary movement', so called, in the hands of an educated class just as does the so-called 'revolutionary party.'

'Spontaneity' (sometimes nowadays mixed up with autonomy) means that the workers are only expected to come in the fray when there's any fighting to be done, and in the normal times leave theorising to the specialists or students. One does not, understandably, find many workers going along with these views which are more popular with students/intelligentsia who espouse the 'marginals' as the new vanguards.

FEMINIST ARGUMENTS FOR AND AGAINST ANARCHISM

The written tradition of Anarchism has not dealt with women's position in society in any depth. Proudhon said 'Women are only fit to be housewives and courtesans.' Proudhon did contribute to Anarchist thinking. However, Anarchism is not based on any one person's ideas, but on practical plans for the reorganisation of society. We take those ideas which we find useful, and discard those which are irrelevant or harmful.

Male domination of groups is a problem as there are more men in many Anarchist groups than women. Mutual aid being a prime aspect of Anarchism, women get especially angry when they see men who aren't sensitive to looking after children, responsibility for people's well-being, etc.

Women need to get stronger and break out of conditioned passivity, by organising together, in mixed groups, and daily life, and in solidarity with each other. Men need to break their male conditioning – becoming more aware, sensitive and put mutual aid into practice to make everyday survival easier all round.

Ideally any attempt at control by dominant personalities, usually male, should be confronted and fought – easier said than done!

A common feminist misconception is that the only way to change society is from a position of power, in a political party, on 'womens' committees' in local government, etc. Anarchists are criticised for working for the overthrow of Statism, by those with party or local government careers.

Right wing governments have never hesitated to put women in powerful positions: Indira Gandhi, Sirimavo Bandaranaike, Golda-Meir, Margaret Thatcher, Eva Peron etc.

Another feminist criticism of Anarchism is that Anarchists are violent. Arguments against pacifism are also covered on another page. There is a certain trend within feminism which asserts that women are 'morally superior' to men and confrontational behaviour is equated with machismo. This is an insult to women everywhere who have, at some time, fought back against State violence, to defend their homes, workmates, children, livelihoods and sanity.

Anarchist Feminists look back at our history of fighting Anarchist women, such as Louise Michel and the women incendiaries of the Paris Commune, and Lucy Parsons and Lizzie Swank Holmes who advocated murderous revenge against the exploiters.

THE AVERAGE PERSON'S OBJECTION TO ANARCHISM

Generally speaking the ordinary people pick up their objection to Anarchism from the press, which in turn is influenced by what the Establishment want. For many years there was a press conspiracy of silence against Anarchism, followed in the 1960s by a ruling on transcribing Anarchism and Marxism, or Anarchism and Nationalism, so that the one must be referred to the other, in order to confuse. This was borne out in many exposures in *Black Flag* showing where avowed Marxists were in the turbulent sixties described in the Press as "Anarchists" while avowed Anarchists were described as "Marxists" or "Nationalists". On some occasions Nationalists were called "Anarchists" but usually when the word "Anarchist" was being used it was as if to describe oneself as an Anarchist was to make a confession of guilt. This, as we have seen, is picked up from the liberal-democratic attitude to Anarchism; but it is flavoured strongly with the fascist attitude also. Because of it, the phrase "self-confessed Anarchist" came to be used by the Press to describe a person who is an Anarchist as opposed to someone who they have merely labelled Anarchist in order to confuse.

This has altered somewhat with the commercial exploitation of Anarchism by the music industry and the academic exploitation of philosophy, giving rise to a middle class Liberal version of an Anarchist as a liberal-minded philosopher, a harmless eccentric, a drop out or a person wearing fashionably unfashionable clothes.

As opposed to this increasingly popular misconception, the average person takes the fascist view of Anarchism, as picked up in its entirety by police officers and others, as genuine; but tempered with the fact that they do not take it quite seriously. Sometimes they confuse the word "revolutionary", and assume all who protest are thereby Anarchist. This ignorance, however, is more often displayed by journalists than it is by the general public.

When it comes down to an objection to Anarchism as it is, as distinct from objections to a mythological Anarchism as imagined or caricatured by the authoritarian parties or Establishment, or practised by the Alternative Establishment, there are not many serious objections from the general public. They may not think it as practical or capable of realisation if presented in a positive way to them; but they usually do so if presented in a negative way – i.e. describing the tyranny of the State, The fact that we could dispense with authoritarian parties, the worthlessness of politicians and so on, is generally agreed. The sole main objection is perhaps the feeling that they want to make the best out of life as it is; and they do not feel strong enough to challenge the State or to face the struggle involved in bringing about a free society, or put up with the many vicissitudes major and minor, that make up the life of a militant or someone reasonably committed to an ideal. The temptations to conform and to accept the bribes which the capitalist class can now hold out are great. Only when the State wants its last ounce of blood do people wake up to the need for resistance, but then it is too late, and also, of course, the State then takes on the pretence of being "the country" in order to be loved instead of hated or disliked.

THE REDUCTION OF ANARCHISM TO MARGINALISATION

By crafty methods, not used against other political theories, it is endeavoured by Statist propaganda to marginalise Anarchism to nothing. It is confused by journalists, professors and subsidised "researchers" to show that Anarchists are identical to drop-outs, drug-takers, nationalist assassins, New Age travellers, political dissidents, militant trade unionists, young rebels, middle-class theorists, dreamers, plotters, comedians, frustrated reformers, extreme pacifists, murderers, schoolboy rebels and criminals. Some Anarchists, one supposes, could be any but hardly all of these, as could members of all political persuasions, but none could be descriptive of the Cause. By misuse of the word "Anarchist" or by added "alleged" or "self-confessed" Anarchist; or by conjoining the word with an obvious contradiction, Anarchism can be marginalised and by implication Statist theories made to seem the norm.

Albert Meltzer

Many other books about anarchism as well as others by Albert Meltzer are available from Active Distribution Mailorder.

www.activedistributionshop.org